March of America Facsimile Series

Number 14

The Relation of David Ingram

Richard Hakluyt

The Relation of David Ingram

from The Principall Navigations

by Richard Hakluyt

ANN ARBOR

UNIVERSITY MICROFILMS, INC.

A Subsidiary of Xerox Corporation

Foreword

"The Relation of David Ingram" which Richard Hakluyt included in the 1589 edition of *The Principall Navigations* provided Europeans with their first description of the interior of a great portion of eastern North America. Ingram testified that he had traveled, overland presumably, from the vicinity of the Panuco River on the Gulf of Mexico all the way north to a point near Cape Breton in Nova Scotia. The trip, which began in October, 1568, required eleven months to complete and must have covered a route of not less than 3,000 miles.

David Ingram was one of those who sailed with John Hawkins on his third expedition from England in 1567 for plunder and trade in the New World. When Hawkins' squadron was surprised by a Spanish fleet in the harbor of San Juan de Ulúa, several of his ships were lost. The two ships which escaped from the harbor were so overcrowded with survivors that it was judged best to put some of the men ashore near the Panuco River with a promise to return for them in a year. Those left ashore disagreed about what to do next. Some preferred to head to the south. Others, fearing capture by the Spaniards, struck out to the north. David Ingram with two others made their way to Nova Scotia, where they found a French ship and so obtained a safe passage home.

The route taken by Ingram is uncertain. Sir Francis Walsingham, Queen Elizabeth's Secretary of State, summoned Ingram for questioning about his trip in 1582. Ingram's answers to the questions put to him at the time form the basis of this "Relation." However, Ingram's questioners primarily wanted information which would be useful for colonization in North America and they were interested in Ingram's trip only as it pertained to this purpose.

The answers given by Ingram had limited practical value. His comment that "the ground & Countrey is most excellent, fertile and pleasant," obviously lacked precision because of the vast expanse of territory to which he alluded. Some of his remarks were fanciful. He reported having seen elephants and claimed to have spied "one other strange Beast bigger than a Beare; he had neither head nor necke: his eyes and mouth were in his breast." On the other hand, Ingram's statement that "sometimes of the yeere there are great windes in maner of Whirlewindes," cannot be challenged. There are other remarks about the country and about the Indians which also have a genuine ring.

Evidently Hakluyt had second thoughts about Ingram's "Relation," however, for he dropped it from the 1599 edition of his *Navigations*. Samuel Purchas, who like Hakluyt collected accounts of travel and exploration, also showed a certain skepticism about Ingram when he referred to "incredibilities" in his story. An examination of Ingram's "Relation" is contained in Rayner Unwin, *The Defeat of John Hawkins* (New York, 1960), pp. 293-312.

The Relation of David Ingram

THE PRINCIPALL NAVIGATIONS, VOIAGES AND DISCOVERIES OF THE

English nation, made by Sea or ouer Land,

to the moſt remote and fartheſt diſtant Quarters of
the earth at any time within the compaſſe
of theſe 1500. yeeres : Deuided into three
ſeuerall parts, according to the po-
ſitions of the Regions wherun-
to they were directed.

The firſt, conteining the perſonall trauels of the Engliſh vnto *Iudæa, Syria, A-rabia*, the riuer *Euphrates, Babylon, Balſara*, the *Perſian* Gulfe, *Ormuz, Chaul, Goa, India*, and many Iſlands adioyning to the South parts of *Aſia* : toge-ther with the like vnto *Egypt*, the chiefeſt ports and places of *Africa* with-in and without the Streight of *Gibraltar*, and about the famous Promon-torie of *Buona Eſperanẓa*. .

The ſecond, comprehending the worthy diſcoueries of the Engliſh towards the North and Northeaſt by Sea, as of *Lapland, Scrikſinia, Corelia*, the Baie of *S. Nicholas*, the Iſles of *Colgoicue, Vaigats*, and *Noua Zembla* toward the great riuer *Ob*, with the mightie Empire of *Ruſſia*, the *Caſpian* Sea, *Georgia, Armenia, Media, Perſia, Boghar* in *Bactria*, & diuers kingdoms of *Tartaria*.

The third and laſt, including the Engliſh valiant attempts in ſearching al-moſt all the corners of the vaſte and new world of *America*, from 73. de-grees of Northerly latitude Southward, to *Meta Incognita, Newfoundland*, the maine of *Virginia*, the point of *Florida*, the Baie of *Mexico*, all the In-land of *Noua Hiſpania*, the coaſt of *Terra firma, Braſill*, the riuer of *Plate*, to the Streight of *Magellan*: and through it, and from it in the South Sea to *Chili, Peru, Xaliſco*, the Gulfe of *California, Noua Albion* vpon the backſide of *Canada*, further then euer any Chriſtian hitherto hath pierced.

Whereunto is added the laſt moſt renowmed Engliſh Nauigation,
round about the whole Globe of the Earth.

By Richard Hakluyt Maſter of Artes, and Student ſometime
of Chriſt-church in Oxford.

Ｊmprinted at London by GEORGE BISHOP
and RALPH NEWBERIE, Deputies to
CHRISTOPHER BARKER, Printer to the
Queenes moſt excellent Maieſtie.

1589.

TO THE RIGHT HONO
RABLE SIR FRANCIS WALSINGHAM
Knight, Principall Secretarie to her Maiestie, Chancellor
of the Duchie of Lancaster, and one of her Maiesties
most honourable Priuie Councell.

IGHT Honorable, I do remember
that being a youth, and one of her Maiesties
scholars at Westminster that fruitfull nurse-
rie, it was my happe to visit the chamber of
M. *Richard Hakluyt* my cosin, a Gentleman of
the Middle Temple, well knowen vnto you,
at a time when I found lying open vpon his
boord certeine bookes of Cosmographie,
with an vniuersall Mappe : he seeing me
somewhat curious in the view therof, began
to instruct my ignorance, by shewing me the
diuision of the earth into three parts after
the olde account, and then according to the latter, & better distribution, into
more: he pointed with his wand to all the knowen Seas, Gulfs, Bayes, Straights,
Capes, Riuers, Empires, Kingdomes, Dukedomes, and Territories of ech part,
with declaration also of their speciall commodities, & particular wants, which
by the benefit of traffike, & entercourse of merchants, are plentifully supplied.
From the Mappe he brought me to the Bible, and turning to the 107 Psalme,
directed mee to the 23 & 24 verses, where I read, that they which go downe to
the sea in ships, and occupy by the great waters, they see the works of the Lord,
and his woonders in the deepe, &c. Which words of the Prophet together
with my cousins discourse (things of high and rare delight to my yong nature)
tooke in me so deepe an impression, that I constantly resolued, if euer I were
preferred to the Vniuersity, where better time, and more conuenient place
might be ministred for these studies, I would by Gods assistance prosecute that
knowledge and kinde of literature, the doores whereof (after a sort) were so
happily opened before me.

According to which my resolution, when, not long after, I was remoued to
Christ-church in Oxford, my exercises of duety first performed, I fell to my intended course, and by degrees read ouer whatsoeuer printed or written discoueries and voyages I found extant either in the Greeke, Latine, Italian, Spanish, Portugall, French, or English languages, and in my publike lectures
was the first, that produced and shewed both the olde imperfectly composed,
and the new lately reformed Mappes, Globes, Spheares, and other instruments
of this Art for demonstration in the common schooles, to the singular pleasure,
and generall contentment of my auditory. In continuance of time, and by rea-
son principally of my insight in this study, I grew familiarly acquainted with
the chiefest Captaines at sea, the greatest Merchants, and the best Mariners of
our nation : by which meanes hauing gotten somewhat more then common
knowledge, I passed at length the narrow seas into France with sir *Edward Staf-
ford,* her Maiesties carefull and discreet Ligier, where during my fiue yeeres a-
boad with him in his dangerous and chargeable residencie in her Highnes seruice, I both heard in speech, and read in books other nations miraculously ex-
tolled for their discoueries and notable enterprises by sea, but the English of all
others for their sluggish security, and continuall neglect of the like attempts e-

specially

specially in so long and happy a time of peace, either ignominiously reported, or exceedingly condemned: which singular opportunity, if some other people our neighbors had beene blessed with, their protestations are often and vehement, they would farre otherwise haue vsed. And that the trueth and euidence heerof may better appeare, these are the very words of *Popiliniere* in his booke called *L'Admiral de France*, and printed at Paris. *Fol. 73. pag. 1,2.* The occasion of his speech is the commendation of the Rhodians, who being (as we are) Islanders, were excellent in nauigation, whereupon he woondereth much that the English should not surpasse in that qualitie, in this sort: *Ce qui m'a fait autresfois rechercher les occasions, qui empeschent, que les Anglois, qui ont d'esprit, de moyens, & valeur assez, pour s'aquerir vn grand honeur parmi tous les Chrestiens, ne se font plus valoir sur l'element qui leur est, & doit estre plus naturel qu'à autres peuples : qui leur doiuent ceder en la structure, accommodement & police de nauires : comme i'ay veu en plusieurs endroits parmi eux.* Thus both hearing, and reading the obloquie of our nation, and finding few or none of our owne men able to replie heerin : and further, not seeing any man to haue care to recõmend to the world, the industrious labors, and painefull trauels of our countrey men : for stopping the mouthes of the reprochers, my selfe being the last winter returned from France with the honorable the Lady Sheffield, for her passing good behauior highly esteemed in all the French court, determined notwithstanding all difficulties, to vndertake the burden of that worke wherin all others pretended either ignorance, or lacke of leasure, or want of sufficient argument, whereas (to speake truely) the huge toile, and the small profit to insue, were the chiefe causes of the refusall. I call the worke a burden, in consideration that these voyages lay so dispersed, scattered, and hidden in seuerall hucksters hands, that I now woonder at my selfe, to see how I was able to endure the delayes, curiosity, and backwardnesse of many from whom I was to receiue my originals : so that I haue iust cause to make that complaint of the maliciousnes of diuers in our time, which Plinie made of the men of his age: *At nos elaborata ijs abscondere atq; supprimere cupimus, & fraudare vitam etiam alienis bonis, &c.*

Plinius. lib. 25. cap. 1. Naturalis historiæ.

To harpe no longer vpon this string, & to speake a word of that iust commendation which our nation doe indeed deserue : it can not be denied, but as in all former ages, they haue bene men full of actiuity, stirrers abroad, and searchers of the remote parts of the world, so in this most famous and peerlesse gouernement of her most excellent Maiesty, her subiects through the speciall assistance, and blessing of God, in searching the most opposite corners and quarters of the world, and to speake plainly, in compassing the vaste globe of the earth more then once, haue excelled all the nations and people of the earth. For, which of the kings of this land before her Maiesty, had theyr banners euer seene in the Caspian sea? which of them hath euer dealt with the Emperor of Persia, as her Maiesty hath done, and obteined for her merchants large & louing priuileges? who euer saw before this regiment, an English Ligier in the stately porch of the Grand Signor at Constantinople? who euer found English Consuls & Agents at Tripolis in Syria, at Aleppo, at Babylon, at Balsara, and which is more, who euer heard of Englishman at Goa before now? what English shippes did heeretofore euer anker in the mighty riuer of Plate? passe and repasse the vnpassable (in former opinion) straight of Magellan, range along the coast of Chili, Peru, and all the backside of Noua Hispania, further then any Christian euer passed, trauers the mighty bredth of the South sea, land vpon the Luzones in despight of the enemy, enter into alliance, amity, and traffike with the princes of the Moluccaes, & the Isle of Iaua, double the famous Cape of Bona Speranza, ariue at the Isle of Santa Helena, & last of al returne home most richly ladē with the cõmodities

modities of China, as the subiects of this now florishing monarchy haue done?

Lucius Florus in the very end of his historie *de gestis Romanorum* recordeth as a wonderfull miracle, that the *Seres*, (which I take to be the people of *Cathay*, or *China*) sent Ambassadors to Rome, to intreate frindship, as moued with the fame of the maiesty of the Romane Empire. And haue not we as good cause to admire, that the Kings of the *Moluccaes*, and *Iaua maior*, haue desired the fauour of her maiestie, and the commerce & traffike of her people? Is it not as strãge that the borne naturalles of *Iapan*, and the *Philippinaes* are here to be seene, agreeing with our climate, speaking our language, and informing vs of the state of their Easterne habitations? For mine owne part, I take it as a pledge of Gods further fauour both vnto vs and them: to them especially, vnto whose dootes I doubt not in time shalbe by vs caried the incomparable treasure of the trueth of Christianity, and of the Gospell, vvhile vve vse and exercise common trade with their marchants. I must confesse to haue read in the excellent history intituled *Origines* of *Ioannes Goropius*, a testimonie of king *Henrie* the viij. a prince of noble memory, vvhose intention vvas once, if death had not preuented him, to haue done some singular thing in this case: vvhose vvords speaking of his dealing to that end with himselfe, he being a stranger, & his history rare, I thought good in this place verbatim to record: *Ante viginti & plus eo annos ab Henrico* Ioā. n̄ s Goropiǰ
Becā: originū
lib.5.pag.494.
Kneuetto Equite Anglo nomine Regis Henrici arram accepi, qua conuenerat, Regio sumptu me totam Asiam, quoad Turcorum & Persarum Regum commendationes, & legationes admitterentur, peragraturum. Ab his enim duobus Asiæ principibus facile se impetraturum sperabat, vt non solùm tutò mihi per ipsorum fines liceret ire, sed vt commendatione etiam ipsorum ad confinia quoque daretur penetrare. Sumptus quidem non exiguus erat futurus, sed tanta erat principi cognoscendi auiditas, vt nullis pecunijs ad hoc iter necessarijs se diceret parsurum. O Dignum Regia Maiestate animum, O me fœlicem, si Deus non antè & Kneuettum & Regem abstulisset, quàm reuersus ab hac peregrinatione fuissem, &c. But as the purpose of Dauid the king to builde a house and temple to God was accepted, although Salomon performed it: so I make no question, but that the zeale in this matter of the aforesaid most renowmed prince may seeme no lesse worthy (in his kinde) of acceptation, although reserued for the person of our Salomon her gratious Maiesty, whome I feare not to pronounce to haue receiued the same Heroicall spirit, and most honorable disposition, as an inheritance from her famous father.

Now wheras I haue alwayes noted your wisdome to haue had a speciall care of the honor of her Maiesty, the good reputation of our country, & the aduancing of nauigation, the very walles of this our Island, as the oracle is reported to haue spoken of the sea forces of Athens: and whereas I acknowledge in all dutifull sort how honorably both by your letter and speech I haue bene animated in this and other my trauels, I see my selfe bound to make presentment of this worke to your selfe, as the fruits of your owne incouragements, & the manifestation both of my vnfained seruice to my prince and country, and of my particular duty to your honour: which I haue done with the lesse suspition either of not satisfying the world, or of not answering your owne expectation, in that according to your order, it hath passed the sight, and partly also the censure of the learned phisitian M. Doctor Iames, a man many wayes very notably qualified. Plutarch in the life of Themistocles.

And thus beseeching God, the giuer of all true honor & wisdome to increase both these blessings in you, with continuance of health, strength, happinesse, and whatsoeuer good thing els your selfe can wish, I humbly take my leaue. London the 17 of Nouember.

Your honors most humble alwayes to be
commanded RICHARD HAKLVYT.

I Haue thought it very requiſite for thy further inſtructi-
on and direction in this hiſtorie (Good Reader) to acquaint thee brieflie
with the Methode and order which I haue vſed in the whole courſe thereof: and by the way alſo to let thee vnderſtand by whoſe friendly aide in this
my trauell I haue bene furthered: acknowledging that ancient ſpeach to be
no leſſe true then ingenious, that the offence is great, Non agnoſcere per
quos profeceris, not to ſpeake of them by whom a man in his indeuours is
aſſiſted.

Concerning my proceeding therefore in this preſent worke, it hath bene this. Whatſoeuer teſtimonie
I haue found in any authour of authoritie appertaining to my argument, either ſtranger or naturall, I
haue recorded the ſame word for word, with his particular name and page of booke where it is extant.
If the ſame were not reduced into our common language, I haue firſt expreſſed it in the ſame termes
wherein it is originally written, whether it were a Latine, Italian, Spaniſh or Portingall diſcourſe, or
whatſoeuer els, and thereunto in the next roome haue annexed the ſignification and tranſlation of the
wordes in Engliſh. And to the ende that thoſe men which were the paynefull and perſonall trauellers
might reape that good opinion and iuſt commendation which they haue deſerued, and further, that
euery man might anſwere for himſelfe, iuſtifie his reports, and ſtand accountable for his owne doings,
I haue referred euery voyage to his Author, which both in perſon hath performed, and in writing hath
left the ſame: for I am not ignorant of Ptolomies aſſertion, that Peregrinationis hiſtoria, and not
thoſe wearie volumes bearing the titles of vniuerſall Coſmographie which ſome mē that I could name
haue publiſhed as their owne, beyng in deed moſt vntruly and vnprofitablie ramaſſed and hurled together, is that which muſt bring vs to the certayne and full diſcouerie of the world.

Moreouer, I meddle in this worke with the Nauigations onely of our owne nation: And albeit I
alleage in a few places (as the matter and occaſion required) ſome ſtrangers as witneſſes of the things
done, yet are they none but ſuch as either faythfully remember, or ſufficiently confirme the trauels of
our owne people: of whom (to ſpeake trueth) I haue receiued more light in ſome reſpects, then all our
owne Hiſtorians could affoord me in this caſe, Bale, Foxe, and Eden onely excepted.

And it is a thing withall principally to be conſidered, that I ſtand not vpon any action performed
neere home, nor in any part of Europe commonly frequented by our ſhipping, as for example: Not vpon that victorious exploit not long ſince atchieued in our narow Seas agaynſt that monſtrous Spaniſh
army vnder the valiant and prouident conduct of the right honourable the lord Charles Howard high
Admirall of England: Not vpon the good ſeruices of our two woorthie Generals in their late Portugall expedition: Not vpon the two moſt fortunate attempts of our famous Chieftaine Sir Fraunce
Drake, the one in the Baie of Cales vpon a great part of the enimies chiefeſt ſhippes, the other neere
the Iſlands vpon the great Carrack of the Eaſt India, the firſt (though peraduenture not the laſt) of
that imployment, that euer diſcharged Molucca ſpices in Engliſh portes: theſe (albeit ſingular and
happy voyages of our renowmed countrymen) I omit, as things diſtinct and without the compaſſe of my
preſcribed limites, beyng neither of remote length and ſpaciouſneſſe, neither of ſearch and diſcouerie
of ſtrange coaſts, the chiefe ſubiect of this my labour.

Thus much in breuitie ſhall ſerue thee for the generall order. Particularlie I haue diſpoſed and di-
geſted the whole worke into 3. partes, or as it were Claſſes, not without my reaſons. In the firſt I haue
martialled all our voyages of any moment that haue bene performed to the South and Southeaſt parts
of the world, by which I chiefly meane that part of Aſia which is neereſt, and of the reſt hithermoſt towards vs: For I find that the oldeſt trauels as well of the ancient Britains, as of the Engliſh, were ordinarie to Iudea which is in Aſia, termed by them the Holy land, principally for deuotions ſake according
to the time, although I read in Ioſeph Bengorion a very authenticall Hebrew author, a teſtimonie
of the paſſing of 20000. Britains valiant ſouldiours, to the ſiege and fearefull ſacking of Ieruſalem vnder the conduct of Veſpaſian and Titus the Romane Emperour, a thing in deed of all the reſt moſt ancient. But of latter dayes I ſee our men haue pierced further into the Eaſt, haue paſſed downe the
mightie riuer Euphrates, haue ſayled from Balſara through the Perſian gulfe to the Citie of Ormuz,
and from thence to Chaul and Goa in the Eaſt India, which paſſages written by the parties themſelues
are herein to be read. To theſe I haue added the Nauigations of the Engliſh made for the parts of A-
frica, and either within or without the ſtreights of Gibraltar: within, to Conſtantinople in Romania,
to Alexandria, and Cayro in Egypt, to Tunez, to Goletta, to Malta, to Algier, and to Tripolis in Bar-
bary: without, to Santa Cruz, to Aſafi, to the citie of Marocco, to the Riuer of Senega, to the Iſles of

Cape

Cape Verde, to Guinea, to Benyn, and round about the dreadfull Cape of Bona Speranza, as farre as Goa.

The north, and Northeasterne voyages of our nation I haue produced in the second place, because our accesse to those quarters of the world is later and not so auncient as the former: and yet some of our trauailes that way be of more antiquitie by many hundred yeeres, then those that haue bene made to the westerne coastes of America. Vnder this title thou shalt first finde the old northerne Nauigations of our Brittish Kings, as of Arthur, of Malgo, of Edgar Pacificus the Saxon Monarch, with that also of Nicholaus de Linna vnder the north pole: next to them in consequence, the discoueries of the bay of Saint Nicholas, of Colgoieue, of Pechora, of the Isles of Vaigats, of Noua Zembla, and of the Sea eastwards towardes the riuer of Ob: after this, the opening by sea of the great Dukedome, and Empire of Russia, with the notable and strange iourney of Master Ienkinson to Boghar in Bactria. Whereunto thou maist adde sixe of our voyages eleuen hundred verstes vp against the streame of Dwina to the towne of Vologhda: thence one hundred, and foure score verstes by land to Yeraslaue standing vpon the mighty riuer of Volga: there hence aboue two thousand and fiue hundred versts downe the streame to the ancient marte Towne of Astracan, and so to the manifolde mouthes of Volga, and from thence also by ship ouer the Caspian sea into Media, and further then that also with Camels vnto Georgia, Armenia, Hyrcania, Gillan, and the cheefest Cities of the Empire of Persia: wherein the Companie of Moscouie Marchants to the perpetuall honor of their Citie, and societie, haue performed more then any one, yea then all the nations of Europe besides: which thing is also acknowledged by the most learned Cosmographers, and Historiographers of Christendome, with whose honorable testimonies of the action, not many for number, but sufficient for authoritie I haue concluded this second part.

Touching the westerne Nauigations, and trauailes of ours, they succeede naturallie in the third and last roome, forasmuch as in order and course those coastes, and quarters came last of all to our knowledge and experience. Herein thou shalt reade the attempt by Sea of the sonne of one of the Princes of Northwales, in sayling and searching towards the west more then 400. yeeres since: the offer made by Christopher Columbus that renowned Genouoys to the most sage Prince of noble memorie King Henrie the 7. with his prompt and cheerefull acceptation thereof, and the occasion whereupon it became fruitlesse, and at that time of no great effect to this kingdome: then followe the letters Patentes of the foresaid noble Prince giuen to Iohn Cabot a Venetian and his 3. sonnes, to discouer & conquer in his name, and vnder his Banners vnknowen Regions: who with that royall incouragement & contribution of the king himselfe, and some assistance in charges of English Marchants departed ‖ with 5. sailes Robert Fabian. from the Port of Bristoll accompained with 300. Englishmen, and first of any Christians found out that mightie and large tract of lande and Sea, from the circle Arcticke as farre as Florida, as appeareth in the discourse thereof. The triumphant raigne of King Henry the 8. yelded some prosecution of this discouerie: for the 3. voyages performed, and the 4. intended for all Asia by his Maiesties selfe, do approoue and confirme the same. Then in processe of yeeres ariseth the first English trade to Brasill, the first passing of some of our nation in the ordinarie Spanish fleetes to the west Indies, and the huge Citie of Mexico in Noua Hispania. Then immediatlye ensue 3. voyages made by M. Iohn Hawkins now Knight, then Esquire, to Hispaniola, and the gulfe of Mexico: vpon which depende sixe verie excellent discourses of our men, whereof some for 15. or 16. whole yeeres inhabited in New Spaine, and ranged the whole Countrie, wherein are disclosed the cheefest secretes of the west India, which may in time turne to our no smal aduantage. The next leaues thou turnest, do yeelde thee the first valiant enterprise of Sir Francis Drake vpon Nombre de Dios, the mules laden with treasure which he surprised, and the house called the Cruzes, which his fire consumed: and therewith is ioyned an action more venterous then happie of Iohn Oxnam of Plimmouth written, and confessed by a Spanyard, which with his companie passed ouer the streight Istme of Darien, and building certaine pinnesses on the west shoare, was the first Englishman that entered the South sea. To passe ouer Master Frobisher and his actions, which I haue also newly though briefely printed, and as it were reuiued, whatsoeuer Master Iohn Dauis hath performed in continuing that discouery, which Master Frobisher began for the nothwest passage, I haue faithfully at large communicated it with thee, that so the great good hope, & singular probabilities & almost certaintie therof, which by his industry haue risen, may be knowen generally of all men, that some may yet still prosecute so noble an action. Sir Humfrey Gilbert, that couragious Knight, and very expert in the mysteries of Nauigation amongst the rest is not forgotten: his learned reasons & arguments for the proofe of the passage before named, together with his last more commendable resolution then fortunate successe, are here both to be read. The continuance of the historie, produceth the beginnings, and proceedings of the two English Colonies planted in Virginia at the charges of sir Walter Raleigh, whose entrance vpon those newe inhabitations had bene happie, if it had ben as seriously followed, as it was cheerefully vndertaken. I could not omit in this parte

the

the two voyages made not long since to the Southwest, whereof I thinke the Spanyard hath had some knowledge, and felt some blowes: the one of *Master* Edward Fenton, and his consort *Master* Luke Warde: the other of *Master* Robert Withrington, and his hardie consort *Master* Christopher Lister as farre as 44. degrees of southerly latitude, set out at the direction and charge of the right honorable the Earle of *Cumberland,* both which in diuers respectes may yelde both profite and pleasure to the reader, being carefully perused.

For the conclusion of all, the memorable voyage of *Master* Thomas Candish *into the South sea,* and from thence about the globe of the earth doth satisfie mee, and I doubt not but will fully content thee: which as in time it is later then that of Sir Frauncis Drake, so in relation of the Philippinaes, Iapan, China, and the Isle of S. Helena it is more particular, and exact: and therfore the want of the first made by Sir Frauncis Drake will be the lesse: wherein I must confesse to haue taken more then ordinarie paines, meaning to haue inserted it in this worke: but being of late (contrary to my expectation) seriously delt withall, not to anticipate or preuent another mans paines and charge in drawing all the seruices of that worthie Knight into one volume, I haue yeelded vnto those my freindes which pressed me in the matter, referring the further knowledge of his proceedinges, to those intended discourses.

Now for the other part of my promise, I must craue thy further patience frendly reader, and some longer suspence from the worke it selfe, in acquainting thee with those vertuous gentlemen, and others which partly for their priuate affection to my selfe, but chiefely for their deuotion to the furtherance of this my trauaile, haue yelded me their seuerall good assistances: for I accompt him vnworthy of future fauours, that is not thankefull for former benefites. In respect of a generall incouragement in this laborious trauaile, it were grosse ingratitude in mee to forget, and wilfull maliciousnes not to confesse that man, whose onely name doth carrie with it sufficient estimation and loue, and that is *Master* Edward Dier, of whom I will speake thus much in few wordes, that both my selfe and my intentions herein by his frendly meanes haue bene made knowne to those, who in sundrie particulars haue much steeded me. More specially in my first part, *Master* Richard Staper *Marchant of London,* hath furnished me with diuers thinges touching the trade of Turkie, and other places in the East. *Master* William Burrowgh, *Clarke of her Maiesties nauie,* and *Master* Anthonie Ienkinson, both gentlemen of great experience, and obseruations in the north Regions, haue much pleasured me in the second part. In the third and last besides myne owne extreeme trauaile in the histories of the Spanyards, my cheefest light hath bene receiued from Sir Iohn Hawkins, Sir Walter Raleigh, and my kinseman *Master* Richard Hakluyt of the middle Temple.

And whereas in the course of this history often mention is made of many beastes, birds, fishes, serpents, plants, fruits, hearbes, rootes, apparell, armour, boates, and such other rare and strange curiosities, which wise men take great pleasure to reade of, but much more contentment to see: herein I my selfe to my singuler delight haue bene as it were rauished in beholding all the premisses gathered together with no small cost, and preserued with no litle diligence, in the excellent Cabinets of my very worshipfull and learned friends M. Richard Garthe, one of the Clearkes of the pettie Bags, and M. William Cope *Gentleman Vssier to the right Honourable and most prudent Counseller* (the Seneca of our common wealth,) the Lord Burleigh, high Treasourer of England.

The excellent newe Globe of M. Mullineux.

Nowe, because peraduenture it would bee expected as necessarie, that the descriptions of so many parts of the world would farre more easily be conceiued of the Readers, by adding Geographicall, and Hydrographicall tables thereunto, thou art by the way to be admonished that I haue contented my selfe with inserting into the worke one of the best generall mappes of the world onely, vntill the comming out of a very large and most exact terrestriall Globe, collected and reformed according to the newest, secretest, and latest discoueries, both Spanish, Portugall, and English, composed by M. Emmerie Mollineux of Lambeth, a rare Gentleman in his profession, being therein for diuers yeeres, greatly supported by the purse and liberalitie of the worshipfull marchant M. William Sanderson.

This being the summe of those things which I thought good to admonish thee of (good Reader) it remaineth that thou take the profite and pleasure of the worke: which I wish to bee as great to thee, as my paines and labour haue bene in bringing these rawe fruits vnto this ripenesse, and in reducing these loose papers into this order. Farewell.

The Relation of Dauid Ingram of Barking, in the Countie of Essex Sayler, of sundry things which he with others did see, in traueiling by land from the most Northerly partes of the Baie of Mexico (where he with many others were set on shoare by Master Hawkins) through a great part of America, vntill he came within fiftie leagues or there abouts of Cape Britton.

Bout the beginning of October, Anno 1568. Dauid Ingram with the rest of his company being 100. persons in all, were set on land by M. Iohn Hawkins, about sire Leagues to the West of the riuer La mina, or Rio de Minas, which standeth about 140. leagues west & by North from the cape of Florida, who traueling towards cape Britton, spent about 12. moneths in the whole, And about seuen moneths thereof in those Countries, which lie towards the North of the riuer of May, in which time (as the said Ingram thinketh) he traueiled by land two thousand miles at the least, and neuer continued in any one place aboue three or foure dayes, sauing onely at the Citie of Balma, where he stayed sire or seuen dayes.

Kings.   There are in those partes (sayth he) very many Kings, commonly within a hundreth or a hundreth and twenty miles one from an other, who are at continual warres together: The first King that they came before, dwelt in a Countrey called Giricka, who caused them to be stripped naked, and wondring greatly at the whitenes of their skins, let them depart without further harme.

Large precious stones.   The Kings in those Countries are clothed with painted or colloured garments, and thereby you may know them, and they weare great precious stones, which commonly are Rubies, being 4. inches long, and two inches broad. And if the same bee taken from them, either by force or sleight, they are presently depriued of their kingdomes.

The Kings in their maiestie.   When they meane to speake with any person publikely, they are alwaies carried by men in a sumptuous chaire of Siluer or Christal, garnished with diuers sortes of precious stones.

The maner of saluting their kings.   And if you will speake with the king at your first approching neere to him, you must kneele downe on both your knees, and then arise againe and come somewhat neerer him, within your length, thē kneele downe againe as you did before. Then take of the earth or grasse between both your hands, kissing the backside of each of them, and put the earth or grasse on the crowne of your head, and so come, & kisse the kings feete. Which circumstances being perfourmed, you may then arise and stand vp, and talke with him.

How to know the noble men.   The Noble men and such as be in special fauour with the King, do commonly weare feathers in the haire of their heads for the most part, of a Byrde, as bigge as a goose of russet collour. And this is the best marke that this Ingram can giue to know him by.

Pearle.   There is in some of those Countries great aboundance of pearle, for in euery cottage he found pearle, in some houses a quart, in some a pottle, in some a pecke, more or lesse, where he did see some as great as a beane. And Richard Browne one of his companions, found one of these great pearles in one of their Canoes or boats, which pearle he gaue to Mounsier Campain, who tooke them aboard his ship, and brought them to Newhauen in France,

Bracelets of Gold.   All the people generally do weare Manilios or Bracelets, as big as a mans finger, vpon each

of

of their armes, and the like on the small of eche of their legs, whereof commonly one is golde and two siluer.

And many of the women also doe weare plates of golde, couering their bodies in maner of a payre of curets, and many bracelets and chaines of great pearle. *Curets of golde.*

The people commonly are of good fauour, feuter & shape of body, of growth aboue fiue foote high, somewhat thicke, with their faces and skins of colour like an oliefe, and toward the North somewhat tawnie, but some of them are painted with diuers colours, they are very swift of foote, the haire of their heads is shauen in sundry spots, and the rest of their head is traced. *The fauour and shape of the people.*

In the South partes of these countreys they go all naked, sauing that the Noble mens priuities are couered with the necke of a goorde, and the womens priuities with the hayre or leafe of the palme tree. But in the North partes they are clothed with beastes skins, the hayrie side being next to their bodies in winter. *Naked people.*

They are so brutish & beastly, that they wil not forbeare the vse of their wiues in open presence. *Brutish behauiour.*

They are naturally very courteous, if you do not abuse them, either in their persons or goods, but vse them courteously. The killing or taking of their beasts, birds, fishes, or fruites cannot offende them, except it be of their cattell which they keepe about their houses, as Kine, Guinie hennes, or such like. *People courteous.*

If any of them doe holde vp both their hands at length together, and kisse the backes of them on both sides, then you may vndoubtedly trust them, for it is the greatest token of friendship that may be. *A sure token of friendship.*

If any of them shal come vnto you with a horsetaile in his hand, then you may assure your selfe that hee is a Messenger from the King, and to him you may safely commit your person, or go to the king, or any where els, or by him send any thing or message to the king. For these men are alwayes either Ensigne bearers in the warres, or the kings messengers, who wil neuer betray you. *Messengers from the king.*

If you will haue any of the people come aborde your ship, hang out some white cloth vpon a staffe, for that is a signe of amitie. *To allure the people to speach.*

If you will bargaine for ware with them, leaue the thing that you will sell vpon the ground, and go from it a prettie way of: then wil they come and take it, and set downe such wares as they will giue for it in the place: And if you thinke it not sufficient, leaue the wares with signes that you like it not, and they will bring more, vntill either they or you be satisfied, or will giue no more. Otherwise you may hang your wares vpon a long poles end, and so put more or lesse on it, vntill you haue agreed on the bargaine. *The maner of trafique and dealing with them.*

When they goe to the warres, they march in battell aray two and three in a ranck. *Howe they march in battell.*

Their Trumpets they doe make of certaine beasts teeth, they haue a kinde of Drum which they make of beastes skins, they make shields and Targets of the skins of beastes, compassed with willowe twigs, and being dried, they are strong and defensible. *Their weapons and instruments for warre.*

Their weapons are dartes, headed with yron, the heads are two fingers broad, and halfe a foot long, which are fastened within a socket.

They haue also short bowes, strung with ye barke of trees, being halfe an ynch broad, & the arrowes are of bone, a yarde long, nocked and headed with siluer & bone, and their arrowes are of small force within a stones cast of them, and you may put them by with a staffe a prettie way off.

They haue short broad swordes of blacke yron of the length of a yarde, or very neere an elle, bearing edges thicker then backs of kniues, somewhat like the foyles in our fence schooles.

They haue crooked kniues of yron, somewhat like a woodknife, or hanger, wherewith they will carue excellently both in wood and bone.

Their Ensigne is a horse taile, with glasse or Christall in some of them being dyed in sundry colours, as red, yellow, greene, &c.

The people in those Countreys are professed enemies to the Canibals or men eaters: The Canibals doe most inhabite betweene Norumbega, & Bariniah, they haue teeth like dogs teeth, and thereby you may know them. In the warres they doe pitch their campe as neere as they may vnto some wood of Palme tree, which yeelde them meate, drinke, and present remedy against poysoned arrowes. *Canibals.*

Their buildings are weake and of small force, their houses are made round like Doue houses, and they doe dwell together in Townes and Villages. And some of them haue banqueting houses in the top of them, made like the loouer of a hall, builded with pillars of massie siluer, and chrystall, framed square: whereof many of them are as big as a boyes leg of fifteene yeeres of age, and some lesse. *Their houses and buildings.*

This Ingram did also see diuers Townes and Villages, as Gunda, a Towne a flight shoote *Townes and Villages.*

shoote in length.

Ochala, a great Towne a mile long.

Balma, a rich Citie, a mile and a halfe long.

Bega, a Countrey, and Towne of that name, three quarters of a mile long, where are good ftore of Oxe hides.

Saguanah, a Towne almoſt a mile in length.

Bariniah, a Citie a mile and a quarter long : Alfo there is a Riuer and a Towne of that name, but leffe then the firſt aboue named.

Guinda, a ſmall Towne and a Riuer, both of that name. And this is the moſt Northerly part, that this Ingram was at.

There are befides thofe Townes aforenamed, many other great Townes which this Ingram paſſed by, commonly diſtant fixe or eight miles one from the other, which haue diuers ſmall Uillages within eight or ten miles from them.

Veſſels of maſſie ſiluer, for common vſes. They haue in euery houfe fcoupes, buckets, and diuers other veſſels of maſſie ſiluer, wherewith they doe throwe out water and duſt, and otherwiſe doe imploy them to their neceſſary vſes in their houſes : All which this Ingram did ſee common and vfuall in fome of theſe Countreys, eſpecially where he found the great Pearles.

Gold in the heads of Riuers. There are alfo great riuers, at the heads whereof, this Ingram & his companions did find fundry pieces of golde, fome as big as a mans fiſt, the earth being waſhed away with the water.

Rocks of chryſtall. And in other places, they did fee great rockes of Chryſtall, which grewe at the heads of great and many Riuers, being in quantitie to loade ſhippes.

Fine Furres. There are alfo in thofe partes, plentie of fine Furres, vnknowen to this Ingram, dreſſed after the maner of the Countrey.

Sweete turfe to burne. The people there do burne a kind of white Turfe or earth, which they dig out of the mariſhes, a fadome deepe in the ground. It burneth very cleare, and ſmelleth as ſweete as muſke, and that earth is as wholefome, ſweete, and comfortable, to ſmell vnto, as any Pomander. They do make their fire of this earth for the ſweetnes thereof, hauing great aboundance of wood.

Their maner of kindling fire. When they want fire, they take briers, and rub them very hard together betweene their fiſts, and fo with hard and often rubbing they kindle and make fire.

Iron and Minerall ſalt. They haue great plentie of Iron, and there is alfo great plentie of minerall ſalt, in the mariſh ground which looketh reddiſh, a thing neceſſary for the great fiſhings neere the ſea ſhore, which are there aboundant, and the fiſh very large and huge.

The fertilitie of the foyle. The ground & Countrey is moſt excellent, fertile and pleaſant, & ſpecially towards the Riuer of May. For the graſſe of y reſt is not fo greene, as it is in theſe parts, for the other is burnt away with the heate of the Sunne. And as all the Countrey is good and moſt delicate, hauing great **Plaines.** plaines, as large & as fayre in many places as map be feene, being as plaine as a board: And then **Great woods. Palmes.** great & huge woods of fundry kind of trees, as cedar, Lignum vitæ, Bombaſſe, plants & buſſhes, bark that biteth like Pepper, (of which kind, yong M. Winter brought home part from y ſtraight of Magelane) with the fruitfull Palme tree, & great plentie of other ſweete trees to this Ingram **Clofes and paſtures.** vnknowen. And after that plaines againe, and in other places great clofes of paſture, enuironed with moſt delicate trees, in ſtead of hedges: they being as it were fet by the hands of men : Yet the beſt graſſe for the moſt part is in the high Countries, fomewhat farre from the Sea ſide, and great Riuers, by reafon that the lowe grounds there be fo rancke, that the graſſe groweth faſter then it can be eaten, whereby the olde graſſe lieth withered thicke, and the newe graſſe growing through it. Whereas in the vpper partes, the graſſe and ground is moſt excellent and greene. The ground not being ouercharged with any olde withered graſſe, as is afore ſpecified.

The Palme tree. The Palme tree aforeſayd carieth hayres on the leaues thereof, which reach to the ground, Whereof the Indians doe make ropes and cords for their Cotten beds, and doe vfe the fame to many other purpoſes.

Wine of the Palme. The which Tree, if you pricke with your knife, about two foote from the roote, it will yeelde a Wine in colour like whey, but in taſte ſtrong and fomewhat like Baſtard, which is moſt excellent drinke. But it wil diſtemper both your head and body, if you drinke too much thereof, as our ſtrong Wines wil doe in theſe partes.

Meate of the Palme. The branches of y top of y tree, are moſt excellent meat raw, after you haue pared away y bark.

Oyle againſt poyfoned arrowes. Alfo there is a red oyle that commeth out of y roote of this tree, which is moſt excellent againſt poifoned arrowes & weapons: for by it they doe recouer themfelues of their poyfoned wounds.

The Plantine with his fruits There is a tree called a Plantine, with a fruite growing on it like a pudding, which is moſt excellent meate rawe.

They

They haue also a red berry like a Pescod,called Guyathos, two or three ynches long, which groweth on short bushes full of pricks like the Sloe or Thorne tree, and the fruite eateth like a greene Raisin, but sharper somewhat : They stampe this berry and make Wine thereof,which they keepe in vessels made of wood.

They haue also in many places, Vines which beare Grapes as big as a mans thumbe. *Vines with great Grapes.*

There is also great plentie of herbes,and of all kinde of flowers , as Roses , and Gillcflowers,like ours in England,and many others which he knewe not. *Herbes and flowers.*

Also,they haue a kinde of Graine,the eare whereof is as big as the wrist of a mans arme: the Graine is like a flat pease, it maketh very good bread and white. *Graine.*

They doe also make bread of the roote called Cassaua , which they doe drie, and beate it as small as they can,and temper it with water, and so bake it in cakes on a stone. *Bread of a Cassaba.*

There is also great plenty of Buffes,Beares,Horses,Kine,Woolues, Foxes,Deare,Goats, Sheepe, Hares,and Conies : Also other cattell like ours , to this Examinate vnknowen, the most part being wilde : the Hides and skinnes of them are good Marchandize. There is very great store of those Buffes,which are beasts as big as two Oxen,in length almost twentie foot, hauing long eares like a Blood hound,with long haires about their eares,their hornes be crooked like Rams hornes,their eyes blacke, their haires long,blacke,rough, & shagged as a Goat: The Hides of these beasts are solde very deare, this Beast doeth keepe companie onely by couples,male and female,& doeth alwayes fight with others of the same kinde when they do meete. There is also great plentie of Deare both red,white,and speckled. This last sort this Examinate knoweth not. There is also great plentie of another kinde of Sheepe which carie a kinde of course wooll : This Sheepe is very good meate, although the flesh be very red. They are exceeding fatte, and of nature loth to rise when they are laid,which is alwayes from fiue a clocke at night,vntill fiue a clocke in the morning: betweene which time you may easily kill them, but after they be on foote they are very wilde, & rest not in one place,but liue together in heards, in some 500.as it happeneth,more or lesse : And these red Sheepe are most about the Bay of Saint Marie,as this Examinate gesseth. There are Beares both blacke and white. There are Woolues. The Foxes haue their skins more grisled then ours in England. There are Conies both white and red,and grey in euery place great plentie. *Beasts of sundry kindes.* *Vacca gibbosa,supposed a Buffe.* *Deare.* *Sheepe bearing wooll the flesh red.*

This Examinate did also see in those Countries a Monstrous beast twise as big as an Horse, and in proportion like to an Horse,both in maine, hoofe,haire,and neighing,sauing it was small towards the hinder partes like a Grey hound. These Beasts hath two teeth or hornes of a foote long growing straight foorth by their nosethrilles: they are naturall enemies to the Horse. *A strange Beast.*

Hee did also see in that Countrey both Elephants and Ounces. Hee did also see one other strange Beast bigger then a Beare, he had neither head nor necke: his eyes and mouth were in his breast.This beast is very vgly to beholde,and cowardly of kinde. It beareth a very fine skin like a Rat,full of siluer haires. *Elephants and Ounces.* *A strange shapen Beast.*

There are in those Countries abundance of Russet Parrots, but very fewe greene. There are also Birds of all sortes as we haue, and many strange Birds to this Examinate vnknowen. There are great plenty of Guinie hennes which are tame Birds,and proper to the Inhabitants, as big as Geese, very blacke of colour, hauing feathers like Downe. There is also a Bird called a Flamingo,whose feathers are very red,and is bigger then a Goose,billed like a Shouell, and is very good meate. There is also another kinde of Foule in that Countrey which hunteth the Riuers neere vnto the Ilands : They are of the shape and bignesse of a Goose but their wings are couered with small yelowe feathers,and cannot flie: You may driue them before you like sheepe: They are exceeding fatte and very delicate meate,they haue white heads,and therefore the Countrey men call them Penguins(which seemeth to be a Welsh name.)And they haue also in vse diuers other Welsh words, a matter worthy the noting. There is also a very strange Bird,thrise as big as an Eagle, very beautifull to beholde, his feathers are more orient then a Peacockes feathers, his eyes are glistering as an Hawkes eyes , but as great as a mans eyes, his head and thigh as big as a mans head and thigh: It hath a crest and tuffe of feathers of sundry colours on the top of the head like a Lapwing hanging backwards:His beake and talents in proportion like Egles,but very huge and large. *Russet Parots.* *Birds like ours.* *Guinie hens.* *A red Bird.* *Penguins.* *A great strange Bird.*

Touching Tempests and other strange monstrous things in those partes, this Examinate sayth,that he hath seene it Lighten and Thunder in sommer season by the space of foure & twentie houres together: the cause whereof he iudgeth to be the heate of the Climate. *Tempests.*

He farther saith,that there is a Cloud sometime of the yeere seene in the ayre,which commonly turneth to great Tempests. And that sometimes of the yeere there are great windes in maner *Furicanos. Turnados.*

of

of Whirlewindes.

Their maner of Religion.

Touching their Religion, he faith that they honor for their God a Deuil, which they call Colluchio, who fpeaketh vnto them fometimes in the likeneffe of a blacke Dogge, and fometimes in the likeneffe of a blacke Calfe.

And fome doe honor the Sunne, the Moone, and the Starres.

Adulterie punifhed with death.

He faith þ the people in thofe Countries are allowed many Wiues, fome fiue, fome tenne, & a king fometimes an hundred: And þ Adulterie is very feuerely punifhed in maner following, that is to fay: The woman taken in adulterie, muft with her owne hands cut þ throte of the Adulterer, and the next of his kindred doth likewife cut þ throte of the Adultereffe. And being afked in what maner they take their executions, he faith: That they are brought to execution by certaine Magiftrates, who do deliuer vnto þ woman the knife, wherewith fhe cutteth þ throte of the Adulterer.

Then appeareth their Colluchio or Deuil, in the likeneffe aforefaid, and fpeaketh vnto them, and to that Deuil the parties brought to execution doe great reuerence, and with many prayers to it doe take their death.

Their maner of Burials.

He faith that fuch perfons as are put to death in fuch fort, haue not any of their friends buried with them: but fuch as die naturally, haue alwayes buried quicke with them one of their deareft friendes to keepe them companie, and to prouide neceffaries and victuall for them, who doe willingly confent thereto, being thereto perfwaded by their Colluchio or Deuil, whó they do worfhip.

The Deuil fled away at the name of the holy Trinitie.

He faith further, that he & his two fellowes, namely, Richard Browne, and Richard Twide, went into a poore mans houfe, & there they did fee the faid Colluchio or Deuil, with very great eyes like a blacke Calfe: Vpon the fight whereof, Browne faide, There is the Deuil, and therevpon he bleffed himfelfe: In the name of the Father, and of the Sonne, and of the holy Ghoft. And Twide faid very vehemently, I defie thee and all thy workes. And prefently the Colluchio fhrancke away in a ftealing maner forth of the doores, and was feene no more vnto them.

Great Riuers.

Alfo they paffed ouer many great Riuers in thofe Countries, in Canoes or Boates: fome foure, fome fixe, fome eight, fome tenne miles ouer: whereof one was fo large, that they coulde fcarfe croffe the fame in foure and twentie houres.

Muficall inftruments.

Alfo he faith, that in the fame Countrie, the people haue inftruments of Muficke made of a piece of a Cane, almoft a foote long, being open at both endes: which fitting downe, they fmite vpon their thighes and one of their handes, making a pleafant kind of found.

And they do vfe an other kind of inftrument like a Taber, couered with a white fkinne fomewhat like Parchment.

This Examinate can very well defcribe their geftures, dauncing, and fongs.

After long trauaile, the aforefaide Dauid Ingram with his two companions Browne and Twide, came to the head of a riuer called Garinda, which is 60. Leagues Weft fró Cape Britton: where they vnderftood by the people of that Countrey of þ arriuall of a Chriftian. Wherevpon they made their repaire to the Sea fide, and there found a French Captaine named Monfieur Champaigne, who tooke them into his Shippe and brought them vnto Newhauen, & from thence they were tranfported into England, Anno. Dom. 1569.

Siluer in exchange of trifles.

This Monfieur Campaigne, with diuers of his companie was brought into þ Village of Bariniah, about twentie miles vp into the Countrie by þ faid Examinate and his two Companions, by whofe meanes he had a trade with the people of diuers fortes of fine furres, & of great redde leaues of trees almoft a yard long, & about a foote broade, which he thinketh are good for dying.

Alfo the faid Monfieur Champaigne, had there for exchange of trifling wares, a good quantitie of rude, and wrought filuer.

He faith further, that diuers of the faid Frenchmen which were in the faid Shippe called the Gargarine, are yet liuing in Homflewe vpon the coaft of France, as he thinketh, for he did fpeake with fome of them within thefe three yeeres.

About a fourtnight after their comming from Newhauen into England, this faide Examinate and his two companions came to mafter Iohn Hawkins, who had fet them on fhore vpon the Baie of Mexico, and vnto eche of them he gaue a reward.

Richard Browne his companion was flaine about fiue yeeres paft in the Elizabeth of mafter Cockins of London: And Richard Twide his other cópanion died at Ratcliffe in Iohn Sherewoods houfe there, about three yeeres paft.

The language of fome of the Countreis.

    Gwando. Is a worde of Salutation, as among vs: Good morrowe, Good euen, God faue you or fuch like.
    Caricona. A King.
    Caraccona. A Lord.

Fona.

{ Fona. Bread.
{ Carmugnar. The Priuities.
{ Kerucca. The Sunne.

Also the sayd Dauid Ingram traueiling towardes the North, fonnd the maine sea vpon the *The maine* Northside of America, and trauailed in the sight thereof the space of two whole dayes, where *Sea on the* the people signified vnto him, that they had seene shippes on that coast, and did draw vpon the *North parte of America.* ground the shape and figure of shippes, and of their sailes and flagges. Which thing especially proueth the passage of the Northwest, and is agreeable to the experience of Vasques de Corona-do, which found a shippe of China or Cataia vpon the Northwest of America.

Also the sayd examinate sayth, that there is an Iland called Corrasau, and there are in it fiue *Corrasau* or six thousand Indians at the least, and all those are gouerned by one onely Negro, who is but *Iland.* a slaue to a Spaniard. And moreouer the Spanyardes will send but one of their slaues with an hundred or two hundred of the Indians, when they goe to gather golde in the Riuers descen-ding from the mountaines. And when they shal be absent by the space of twentie or thirty dayes at the least, euery one of the Indians will neuerthelesse obey all the Slaues commaundements with as great reuerence, as if he were their naturall King, although there be neuer a Christian neere them by the space of an hundred or two hundred miles: which argueth the great obedience of those people, and how easily they may be gouerned when they be once conquered.